A Field Guide to the Mammals of Singapore

By Anish Banerjee

© Atish Banerjee

Contents   Page Number

Introduction

Mammals are a group of warm-blooded vertebrate animals which are distinguished from other types of animals by several different features such as the possession of hair and fur, the birth of live offspring and the production of milk by females.

Singapore until the early 20th Century was home to some of the world's rarest mammals in the world including tigers, leopards and various species of smaller mammals. However, sadly due to rapid urbanization and poaching, most of these species have become extinct.

Currently, Singapore has about 64 species of mammals including the elusive leopard cat and the graceful dugongs also known as "sea cows". Many of these species such as the Greater Mousedeer and leopard cats were thought to be extinct in Singapore before being rediscovered recently. Meanwhile there are many species of mammals such as the Short-Tailed Mongoose for which officials are unsure of their existence in Singapore. It is very vital to preserve Singapore's forests as they are home to several globally endangered mammals such as Asian Small-Clawed Otters.

Research shows that PU and PT, the CCNR and BTNR are home to most of the rare mammals in Singapore. This is mainly due to the presence of suitable rainforest habitat. The Straits of Singapore seems to be an important area for aquatic mammals in Singapore such as Indo-Pacific Humpback Dolphins and Indo-Pacific Bottlenose Dolphins.

Due to massive amounts of deforestation and loss of habitat in Malaysia, many species of animals, especially birds are seeking refuge in Singapore. There have been a few instances of mammals swimming across the SJ to PU and PT. In the late 20th Century there were a few incidents of elephants swimming across to these islands. There have been instances of Malaysian Tapir also swimming across to PU and Changi. In fact on 24th June 2016, one tapir was spotted in Changi. Furthermore Malaysian Flying Foxes are visiting Singapore more frequently. Although these sightings are extremely rare, in the future Singapore can be expecting more warm-blooded guests as Malaysia is rapidly developing.

Despite Singapore being one of the most urbanized and smallest cities in the world, it still has such a diverse range of biodiversity, thanks to conservation efforts by the Singaporean Government. NParks are brilliantly preserving nature reserves around Singapore and educating the public about Singapore's rich biodiversity. Many other groups such as NSS Vertebrate Study Group and NUS Students are putting tremendous amounts of effort to research about Singapore's biodiversity. Hopefully this will inspire other developed nations to preserve nature.

Using this book as a guide

Scientific/Binominal Name: The scientific name is basically the Latin name of an organism. The first word identifies the genus (a part of the biological classification of an organism) while the second word is the species the organism belong to.

Other Names: Several species are known by various names across the world. Only the most common names of each species will be listed.

Conservation Status: This status is an indication of the rarity of a species globally and it's chances of becoming extinct in the near future. Listed below are the different possible conservation statuses.

- **Extinct (EX)** – No known individuals remaining anywhere in the world
- **Extinct in the wild (EW)** – Known only to survive in captivity
- **Critically endangered (CR)** – Extremely high risk of extinction in the wild
- **Endangered (EN)** – High risk of extinction in the wild
- Vulnerable (VU) – High risk of endangerment in the wild
- **Near threatened (NT)** – Likely to become endangered in the near future
- **Least concern (LC)** – Lowest risk possible. The population is barely shrinking
- **Data deficient (DD)** – Not enough data to make an assessment of its risk of extinction
- **Not evaluated (NE)** – Has not yet been evaluated against the criteria.

Size: Knowing the average size of a species of mammals can be very helpful in identifying the species of an individual. Listed below are common terms used in this book to describe a mammal's size

- **Head-Body Length-** the length of a mammal's from the tip of its head to the base of its tail
- **Tail Length-** the length from the base of a mammal's tail to the tip of the tail
- **Forearm Length-** length of the one end of the forearm of one arm to the other end.

Identification: Generally, mammals are fairly easy to identify by looking at images unlike other types of organisms such as birds, reptiles and fish. However, there are some species such as bats and rats which may look similar. This section highlights the key identification features of each mammal. The subsequent list are some terms used to describe a mammal's anatomy.
- **Patagium** -a fold of skin which connects hind legs with forelimbs of animals
- **Guard Hair-** The outer fur on mammals
- **Dorsal fin** - a singular fin on the back of a fish or marine mammals
- **Muzzle-** the projected part of an animal's face which consists of the mouth and nose
- **Noseleaf -** a leaf-shaped structure on the nose of various bats used for echolocation

Ecology and Behavior: Most mammals are nocturnal while some such as primates are diurnal. Social structure and diet vary amongst species. Solitary mammals tend to be more shy while gregarious mammals such as long-tail macaques can be very aggressive. Listed below are numerous terms which will be used to explain a mammals behavior.

- **Nocturnal**- active during the night
- **Diurnal** - active during the day
- **Crepuscular** - active mainly during twilight (right after dusk and right before dawn)
- **Terrestrial**- animals which generally live on the ground
- **Arboreal**- animals which generally live in trees
- **Monogamous** - live in the same breeding pairs for life
- **Solitary** - generally living alone
- **Gregarious** - social/ living in flocks

Local Status and Range: The local status of animal is the rarity of a species in Singapore at the present moment. The range is the area where this species is found in Singapore. The local status and range of mammals change over time due to rapid urbanization and climate change.. Therefore, this part should only be used as a guideline of a species range and status in Singapore. Listed below are abbreviations for the main areas where mammals in Singapore are found

- **Central Catchment Nature Reserve**- CCNR
- **BTNR Nature Reserve**- BTNR
- **Western Catchment**- WC
- **Pulau Ubin**- PU
- **Pulau Tenkong**- PT
- **Singapore Straits**- SS
- **Straits of Johor**- SJ
- **Garden by the Bay**- GBTB
- **East Coast Park**- ECP
- **Pasir Ris Park** - PRP
- **Sungei Buloh**- SB

Primates

Primates are the most closely related animals to humans in the worlds as human are themselves classified in this Order. These social creatures are generally diurnal barring tarsiers and slow lorises. They are mostly herbivorous but may frequently feast on animal matter.

There are about 300-350 species of primates in the world. Primates are mainly found in tropical areas. Singapore has three species of primates excluding humans which are all unique in their own way.

Banded Leaf Monkey

Scientific Name: *Presbytis femoralis*
Other Names: Banded Surili, Banded Langur
Conservation Status: Near Threatened

Size: Weight: 5.9-8, 2 kg, Head-Body Length: 43-62 Cm, Tail Length: 61cm-83.8cm

Identification: Mostly has black fur on back and sides which makes it easy to identify. Undersides are white. Young can be more whitish.

Ecology and behavior: Banded leaf Monkeys are arboreal and diurnal primates which lives in small families of about 11 induviduals. These monkeys are generally very shy.

Local Status and Range: Very rare. Only about 40-50 induviduals located in the CCNR

(Image Source: Eddy Lee**)**

Sunda Slow Loris

Scientific Name: *Nycticebus coucang*
Other Names: Greater Slow Loris
Conservation Status: Vulnerable

Size: Weight: 599-685g, Head-Body Length: 27-30cm, Tail Length: 3 cm

Identification: This small venomous primate has dense grey to reddish fur with a round head and relatively large eyes. Limbs are slender and tail is short. This is the smallest primate in Singapore.

Ecology and behavior: This arboreal primate is one of the only few species of nocturnal primates. Slow Lorises are generally solitary but sometimes may be monogamous. Slow Lorises are very shy.

Local Status and Range: Rare. This species is sighted infrequently mainly due to its shyness and nocturnal behavior. Mostly restricted to CCNR.

(Image Source: Jareas Chua**)**

Crab-eating Macaque

Scientific Name: *Macaca fascicularis*
Other names: Long-tailed Macaque
Conservation Status: Least Concern

Size: Weight: 5-9 kg (M), 3-6kg (F), Head-Body Length: 38-55cm, Tail: 40-65cm

Identification: Crab-eating Macaques have dark-grey underparts with dark brown upperparts. The tip of this primate's head is light golden. This macaque is fairly small with a relatively long tail. Both genders have cheek whiskers. Males have a moustache unlike females. Males are also slightly larger.

Ecology and behavior: Like most primates, the crab-eating macaques are social animals living in large families which consist of about 3-20 females, their offspring and a few males (generally 1-4 induviduals). These families are female dominated.

Local Status and Range: This is the most common primate in Singapore. This primate can be found in some forested areas around Singapore it is fairly common in the CCNR.

(Image Source: Sakurai Midori**)**

Carnivores

Carnivorous are animals which have a diet consisting only of other organisms. They vary in size and shape. Most species are solitary and are very territorial. Carnivores only account for a small portion of all mammal species but have a fairly large diversity of species ranging from majestic tigers to the elusive civets. Singapore used to be home to a diverse range of carnivores including tigers, leopards and clouded leopards. Sadly, poaching and rapid urbanization has led to the extinction of many of these unique species. Singapore has 7 confirmed species of carnivores currently. Officials are unsure of the existence of a few native species in Singapore such as otter civets.

Asian Leopard Cat

Scientific Name: *Prionailurus bengalensis*
Other Names: None
Conservative Status: Least Concern

Size: Weight: 0.55kg- 3.8kg, Head-Body Length: 38.8cm - 66cm, Tail Length: 17.2-31cm

Identification: A Leopard Cat is the size of an average domestic cat except it is more slender and has longer legs. As its name suggests, Leopard Cat looks fairly similar to a leopard kitten. This species has two black stripes running horizontally from eyes to ears.

Ecology and behavior: Solitary except during breeding season. Leopard Cats are mainly nocturnal and are very shy.

Local Status: This is species is rare especially on the mainland where it can only be found in the WC and CCNR. In PT, leopard cats are thriving with an estimated population of about 40 individuals. PU also has a stable population of Leopard Cats.

(Image Source: Sunny Patil)

Large Indian Civet

Scientific Name: *Viverra zibetha*
Other Names: None
Conservative Status: Vulnerable

Size: Weight: 5-11kg, Head-Body Length: 58-95cm, Tail Length: 30-53cm

Identification: The Large-Indian Civet is distinguishable from other species of civets by its dog-like structure, greyish face and distinct black and white marking on its neck. Other distinct features of this civet includes its dark limbs, a short black and white banded tail and black spotting on its main body.

Ecology and behavior: Like most other species of civet, the Large Indian Civet is generally solitary, nocturnal and territorial. Their range can vary from 1.7 to 5.4 square km. They spend most of their time on the forest floor but are also agile climbers.

Local Status: It is very rare in Singapore as there only have been sighted in the CCNR in 2008.

(Image Source: TonTan Travel**)**

Malayan Civet

Scientific Name: *Viverra tangalunga*
Other Names: Oriental Civet
Conservative Status: Least Concerned

Size: Weight: 1.4kg- 4.5kg, Head-Body Length: Tail Length:

Identification: The Malayan Civet is identifiable by its tawny colored coat which has black spots. On the neck of this civet, there are three black stripes and two white stripes. It also has a tail which is banded in black and white. There is a long black stripe from this civet's shoulders to tail.

Ecology and behavior: These nocturnal mammals are solitary and quite terrestrial.

Local Status: Malayan Civets are very rare in Singapore as it was Last photographed in 2012 by a camera trap in MacRitchie.

(Image Source: Mariomassone**)**

Three-Striped Palm Civet

Scientific Name: *Arctogalidia trivirgata*
Other Names: Small-Toothed Palm Civet
Conservative Status: Least Concern

Size: Weight: 9-14kg, Head-Body Length: 61-96cm, Tail Length: 56-89cm

Identification: As its name suggests, this species of civet has three distinct dark lines from its neck to its rump. It also has a white stripe from the tip of its nose to its forehead. Other features of this civet include a grey head, dark feet and a brown coat.

Ecology and behavior: The Three-Striped Palm Civet is a nocturnal frugivore. Unlike most civets, this species is highly terrestrial.

Local Status: This species is uncommon. There are confirmed reports of this species in BTNR and the CCNRs. These civets are very vocal and are heard regularly but very few sightings have been reported.

(Image Source: Cicada Tree Eco-Place**)**

Common Palm Civet

Scientific Name: *Paradoxurus hermaphroditus*
Other Names: Musang, Toddy Cat, Asian Palm Civet
Conservation Status: Least Concerned

(**Image Source:** Animal Adda**)**

Size: Weight: 2-5kg, Head-Body Length: 43-72cm, Tail Length: 40-66 cm

Identification: The Common Palm Civet is identifiable by its coat which varies in color from rich cream to jet black. It has whitish markings and long pointed ears on a black head. It has a black tail.

Ecology and behavior: The common palm civet is a nocturnal mammal which is solitary and terrestrial

Local Status and Range: Quite common in throughout Singapore especially CCNR.

Asian Small Clawed Otters

Scientific Name: *Aonyx cinerea*
Other Names: Oriental Small Clawed Otters
Conservation Status: Vulnerable

Size: Weight: 1-5.4kg, Head-Body Length: 40-70cm, Tail Length: 30cm

Identification: The Asian Small Clawed Otter is the smallest otter in the world. It has a dark greyish-brown coat. It has a slender and streamline body. As it name suggests, it has small claws and webbed feet. It is separable from the Smooth-Coated otters by its trapezium-shaped nose. It is also significantly smaller.

Ecology and behavior: Asian Small Clawed Otters are mostly nocturnal and live in monogamous pairs with their young.

Local Status and Range: This species is very rare in Singapore and is only found in PU.

(**Image Source:** MPhil)

Smooth Coated Otters

Scientific Name: *Lutrogale perspicillata*
Other Names: None
Conservative Status: Vulnerable

Size: Weight: 7-11kg, Head-Body Length: 59 to 64cm, Tail Length: 37cm

Identification: This species is easily identifiable by its roundish head and tail, smooth grey-brown coat and V-shaped nostrils. Males are slightly larger with a broader face and are more robust looking

Ecology and behavior: These otters are diurnal and generally live in families which consist of a mated pair and their offspring from the previous breeding season. These otters are not very shy and can be quite aggressive if provoked.

Local Status and Range: Smooth Coated Otters an can be found throughout Singapore. They are regularly seen in SB, PRP, ECP and GBTB.

(Image Source: Atish Banerjee**)**

Bats

Bats are the second most common type of mammals in the world with an estimated 1,240 different species which accounts for 20% of all mammal species. They are the only mammals which are truly capable of flying. Bats are nocturnal species which roost throughout the day generally in groups as large as several hundred induviduals. Bats especially fruit-eating bats help disperse seeds and pollinate flowers which is important for the ecosystem to sustain itself.

There are two main suborders of bats - Megachiroptera (megabats) and Microchiroptera (microbats). Megabats are generally larger than microbats (not always). The major distinctions between the two species are
- Microbats use echolocation to move around and hunt while megabats do not.
- Microbats lack under fur. These bats are either completely naked or only have a few guard hairs
- Megabats are generally frugivore and their diet includes fruits, nectar, and pollen while microbats feed mainly on insects, small mammals, fish and frog (sometimes nectar, pollen and fruit)

There are 5 confirmed species of megabats and 19 species of microbats in Singapore. The presence of two species of megabats - Island Flying Fox and Short-nosed Fruit Bat in Singapore need to be confirmed.

Megabats
<u>Common Fruit Bat</u>
Scientific Name: *Cynopterus brachyotis*
Other Names: Lesser Dog-Faced Fruit Bat, Lesser Short-Nosed Fruit Bat, Malaysian Fruit Bat
Conservation Status: Least Concern

Size: Weight: 21-32g, Head-Body Length: 8-9.6cm, Forearm Length: 6-7cm

Identification: This bat is distinguishable by its dog-like face. Overall, these bats are brown. Males have reddish collar while their female counterparts have yellow collars. It has a long muzzle (projected part of the face) without any distinct nose

Ecology and behavior: Common fruit bats roost in groups of 6-12 induviduals. Like most bats, the common fruit bat is nocturnal.

Local Status and Range: Fairly common in most forests and nature reserves and sometimes found in urban areas.

(Image Source: Eddy Lee)

Cave Nectar Bat

Scientific Name: *Eonycteris spelaea*
Other Names: Common Dawn Bat, Lesser Dawn Bat, Common Nectar Bat
Conservation Status: Least Concerned

Size: Weight: 40-60g, Head-Body Length: 8.5-11cm, Forearm Length: 6-7cm

Identification: The elongated muzzle of the Cave Nectar Bat which is adapted to drinking nectar is similar to that of a dog. The upperparts of this bat are grey-brown to dark brown is color. Underparts are paler with a slight tinge of yellow around the neck.

Ecology and behavior: As its name suggests, the Cave Nectar bat feeds on nectar and roosts in caves. This bat roosts in huge groups of up to 50,000 induviduals bats.

Local Status and Range: Cave Nectar Bats were rediscovered in 1990 in SB Nature Reserve. They are not very common. These bats can be mostly seen in and around the CCNR and BTNR.

(Image Source: Eddy Lee**)**

Dagger-toothed Long-nosed Fruit Bat

Scientific Name: *Macroglossus minimus*
Other Names: Long-Tongued Nectar bat, Northern Blossom Bat, Honey Nectar Bat, Lesser Long-Tongued Fruit Bat
Conservation Status: Least Concern

Size: Weight: 12-18g, Head-Body Length: 6-8.5cm, Forearm Length: 5.5-9.2cm

Identification: Dangger-toothed Long-nosed Fruit Bats have relatively large fur on upperparts which is reddish-brown in color. Underparts have paler and shorter fur on underparts. It has a dark brown stripe running down bilaterally from top of its head to neck.

Ecology and behavior: These fruit bats roost either solitary or in small groups.

Local Status and Range: This species is rare in Singapore. It has been recorded in the mangroves of PU, PT and SB.

(Image Source: Wikipedia**)**

Dusky Fruit Bat

Scientific Name: *Penthetor lucasi*
Other Names: Lucas's Short-nosed Fruit Bat
Conservation Status: Least Concern

Size: Weight: 30-40g, Forearm Length: 5.7-6.2cm

Identification: The Dusky Fruit Bat has dark greyish-brown upperparts and pale grey underparts. It has large ears, a long muzzle and pale grey ears with dark edges. It has relatively small tail.

Ecology and behavior: This bat roosts in caves or in rock shelters sometimes in complete darkness. The Dusky Fruit bat has a unique habit of collecting fruits in their roosts before eating it.

Local Status and Range: The Dusky Fruit bat is a rare species of bat in Singapore and is restricted only to BTNR. This bat was thought to be extinct from 1925 till 1995 when it was rediscovered in BTNR.

(Image Source: Sheet Zoom Image)

Malayan Flying Fox

Scientific Name: *Pteropus vampyrus*
Other Names: Large Flying Fox, Kalang, Greater Fruit Bat
Conservation Status: Near Threatened

Size: Weight: 0.65-1.1kg, Head-Body Length: 27-32cm, Forearm Length: 18-22cm

Identification: This is the largest bat in Singapore. Easily identifiable by its massive size. As its name suggests, the flying fox has a fox-like face. It is a tailless bat with long pointy ears. It has distinct wooly hair. Coloration of this bat can vary depending on gender and age. It has long wings which can grow up to 1.5m in length.

Ecology and behavior: Like most species of bat, the flying foxes are very social and live in colonies of up to 100 induviduals. Larger colonies of about 2,000 induviduals have been recorded in the past.

Local Status and Range: Once a common resident, now the Malayan Flying Fox is a rare visitor from Malaysia. They are commonly seen in the CCNR

(Image Source: Francis Yap**)**

Microbats

Glossy Horseshoe Bat

Scientific Name: *Rhinolophus lepidus*
Other Names: Blyth's Horseshoe Bat
Conservation Status: Least Concern

Size: Weight: 5-6g, Head-Body Length: 3.9-4.8cm, Forearm Length: 3.9-4.1cm

Identification: The Glossy Horseshoe Bat has fu varying from grey brown to reddish brown. As its name suggests, it is fairly glossy. It has pale underparts. Its nose leaf has a distinct horseshoe shape, hence its name.

Ecology and behavior: These bats roost either solitarily or in groups varying from three to several hundreds.

Local Status and Range: Fairly common and mainly can be found in the CCNR.

(Image Source: Wildlife Singapore**)**

Greater Woolly Horseshoe Bat

Scientific Name: *Rhinolophus luctus*
Other Names: None
Conservation Status: Least Concern

Size: Weight: 25-32g, Forearm Length: 5.8-8cm

Identification: The Woolly Horseshoe Bat is the largest Horseshoe Bat in the world and it has grey-brown upperparts and white-grey underparts. This bat has long and fluffy fur. This bat has medium sized ears. Juveniles are darker than adults.

Ecology and behavior: Woolly Horseshoe Bat roosts in pairs or solitary. This bat roosts in cave and hollow trees.

Local Status and Range: This species is rare in Singapore. It can be found in Changi and the CCNR.

(Image Source: Paul Kvartalynov**)**

Trefoil Horseshoe Bat

Scientific Name: *Rhinolophus trifoliatus*
Other Names: None
Conservation Status: Least Concern

Size: Weight: 18-20g, Head-Body Length: 6-6.4cm, Forearm Length: 4-5.7cm

Identification: Trefoil Horseshoe Bats are easily identifiable by its unique yellow noseleaf. It has relatively large yellow ears. This bat has greyish brown fur with reddish brown wings.

Ecology and behavior: This species of bat roost alone. These bats roost on small trees and vines very close to the ground.

Local Status and Range: This species is very rare in Singapore. Sightings of the Trefoil Horseshoe Bat have been recorded only in PT and the CCNR.

(**Image Source:** Wildlife Singapore)

Bicolored Leaf-nosed Bat

Scientific Name: *Hipposideros bicolor*
Other Names: Bicolored Roundleaf Bat
Conservation Status: Least Concern

Size: Weight 8.1g, Forearm Length: 4-5.7cm

Identification: Some unique features of this bat include it pointed ears and its small, pink noseleaf which is a flap of skin on the nose. Bicolored Leaf-nosed Bats are orange in color

Ecology and behavior: This species of bat is an insectivore which feeds near the forest floor of the rainforest. Bicolored Leaf-nosed Bats roost in groups of up to 150 induviduals.

Habitat: Rainforests

Local Status and Range: Bicolored Leaf-Nosed Bats are very rare in Singapore and are restricted only to BTNR. There were no records of this bat for over a century after its original record in 1878. It was rediscovered recently in 2008 in BTNR.

(**Image Source:** Wildlife Singapore)

Malayan False Vampire

Scientific Name: *Megaderma spasma*
Other Names: Lesser False Vampire, Common Asian Ghost Bat
Conservation Status: Least Concern

Size: Weight: Up to 34g ,Head-Body Length: 5.4-8.1cm, Forearm Length: 6.5-7.2cm

Identification: The Malayan False Vampire Bat is dark brown. It has tall ears. Underparts are pal with a whitish belly. This bat has a hairy face. The Malayan False Vampire bat has a short and broad noseleaf which is heart shaped at the base.

Ecology and behavior: These bats roost in colonies of up to 27 induviduals. This species of bat flies very close to the ground.

Local Status and Range: Rare in Singapore. Only found in PU and PT.

(Image Source: Wildlife Singapore**)**

Lesser Sheath-tailed Bat

Scientific Name: *Emballonura monticola*
Other Names: None
Conservation Status: Least Concern

Size: Weight: 5.5g , Forearm Length: 4.3-4.7cm

Identification: This bat has dark to reddish-brown fur. It also has narrow wings and triangular shaped ears. It has a short tail which disappears into its sheath once legs are stretched out.

Ecology and behavior: This bat roosts near cave entrances and large tree holes in groups of more than 20 induviduals.

Local Status and Range: Lesser Sheath-tailed Bats are rare in Singapore and their range is restricted to BTNR.

(Image Source: Eddy Lee**)**

Black-bearded Tomb Bat

Scientific Name: *Taphozous melanopogon*
Other Names: None
Conservation Status: Least Concern

Size: Weight: 24-27g , Head-body length: 9-10cm, Forearm Length: 6-6.8cm

Identification: The Black-bearded Tomb Bat has pale wings which appear whitish in flight. Upperparts of this bat can vary from grey-brown to brown. Underparts are paler than upperparts and are almost completely white. Males have a distinct black beard.

Ecology and behavior: This bat roost on the surface of walls in urban areas and large rocks in forests.

Local Status and Range: This species of bat is very rare in Singapore. There are only two known roosting areas of this species of bat - the basements of a building in Orchard Road and Crawford Street

(Image Source: Aditiya Joshi**)**

Naked-Rumped Pouched Bat

Scientific Name: *Saccolaimus saccolaimus*
Other Names: Pouched-Tomb Bat
Conservation Status: Least Concern

Size: Weight: Around 60g, Head-Body Length: 8-9cm, Forearm Length: 7.6-8.2cm

Identification: Naked-Rumped Pouched Bats have dark reddish to blackish brown upperparts and white underparts. It also has short ears which are broadly rounded. Long narrow wings have black skin with small white portions.

Ecology and behavior: This species of bats roost in colonies varying in size from just a few induviduals to a few hundred bats. Naked-Rumped Pouched Bats are insectivorous bats which are known to hunt together with swiftlets (type of bird) at a maximum of 40m above the ground.

Habitat: Cities, villages, forest edges, cultivated areas and mountainous areas

Local Status and Range: Naked-Rumped Pouched Bats are fairly common and widespread in Singapore especially in the CCNR and BTNRs. This bat was rediscovered in PU in 1993.

(Image Source: Chan Kwok Wai**)**

Malaysian Slit-faced Bat

Scientific Name: *Nycteris tragata*
Other Names: Southeast Asian Hollow-faced Bat
Conservation Status: Least Concern

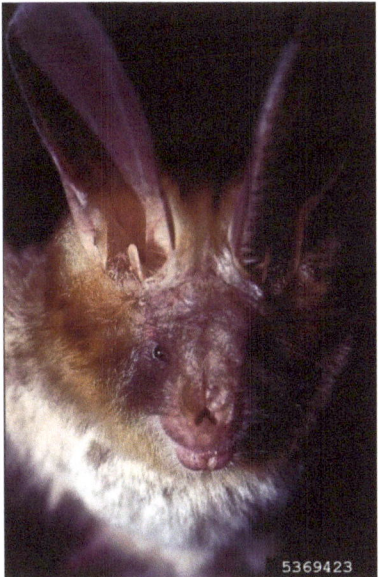

(Image Source: Susan Ellis**)**

Size: Weight: Up to 17g , Forearm Length: Up to 5.1cm

Identification: The Malaysian Slit-faced bat is named after the deep hollow group in the middle of this bat's face. The long and fluffy fur of this bat is reddish brown to grey-brown. This bat has grey-brown ears and noseleaf.

Ecology and behavior: This nocturnal mammal is quite terrestrial and roosts in small groups in caves and hollow trees. Not much is known about this species' ecology.

Local Status and Range: This species is extremely rare in Singapore. Their range is restricted to the CCNR.

Greater Naked Bat

Scientific Name: *Cheiromeles torquatus*
Other Names: Naked Bulldog Bat, Hairless Bat
Conservation Status: Least Concern

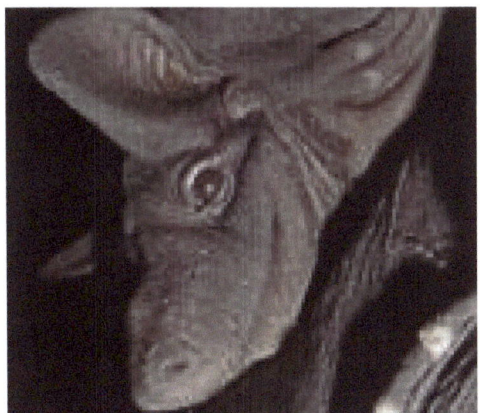

Size: Weight: 180-196g ,Head-Body Length: 12.5-14cm, Forearm Length: 7.7-8.2cm

Identification: The most unique feature of the Greater Naked Bat is its black furless body. Its dog-like face has triangular ears which are forward pointed. This bat has long narrow wings and a thick tail which is very visible even during flight. These bats have relatively large feet with long claws.

Ecology and behavior: The Greater Naked Bat roosts in groups less than 10 induviduals to up to 1000 bats.

Local Status and Range: Not very common in Singapore. It has been sighted mainly around the CCNR and BTNRs and surrounding areas.

(Image Source: Wildlife Singapore**)**

Hardwicke's Woolly Bat

Scientific Name: *Kerivoula hardwickii*
Other Names: Common Woolly Bat, Hardwicke's Forest Bat
Conservation Status: Least Concern

Size: Weight: 3.8-4.4g , Forearm Length: 3.1-3.6cm

Identification: Upperparts of this bat is brownish with lighter greyish brown underparts. Wings are blackish brown. These bats have funnel-shaped noses. Hardwicke's woolly bats are relatively small bats.

Ecology and behavior: Common Woolly bats roost in small tree holes or in hanging vegetation such as dead leaves. Generally they roost solitarily or in small groups.

Local Status and Range: This species is slightly rare in Singapore. Its range is restricted to the CCNR Reserve.

(Image Source: Reddit)

Brown Tube-nosed Bat

Scientific Name: *Murina suilla*
Other Names: Lesser Tube-Nosed Bat
Conservation Status: Least Concern

Size: Weight: 2.5-5.5g, Head-Body Length: 3.2-4.2cm,
Forearm Length: 2.5-3.2cm

Identification: The Brown Tube-Nosed Bat is a fairly small bat with long brown fur. The sides and belly of this bat is grey-brown. The wings of this species are short and rounded.

Ecology and behavior: This bat roosts in medium sized groups in leaf litter, trees and caves.

Local Status and Range: Very rare with only a few sightings in PT.

(Image Source: Tigga Kingston)

Horsfield's Large-footed Myotis

Scientific Name: *Myotis horsfieldii*
Other Names: Horsfield's Bat, Common Asiatic Myotis, Lesser Large-tooth Bat
Conservation Status: Least Concern

Size: Weight:, Head-Body Length:, Forearm Length: 3.4-3.9cm

Identification: The Horsfield's Large-footed Myotis is identifiable by its greyish brown upperparts and grey to dark grey underparts.

Ecology and behavior: These bats roost in caves and underground tunnels. Roosts are generally small but can occasionally have more than 100 induviduals.

Local Status and Range: The Horsfield's Large-Footed Myotis was first discovered in Singapore in 2006 in Upper Pierce Reservoir. This species is fairly rare and is restricted to the CCNR.

(Image Source: マレーシア**)**

Grey Large-footed Myotis

Scientific Name: *Myotis macropus*
Other Names: Southern Myotis
Conservation Status: Least Concern

Size: Weight: 15g ,Head-Body Length: , Wingspan: 28cm, Forearm Length: 3.5-4.3cm

Identification: As its name suggests, the Large-footed Myotis has enlarged feet. Upperparts and sides vary in color from olive- grey to brown while underparts are light grey to white. These bats have large rounded ears.

Ecology and behavior: Large footed Myotis are most active at dusk as during this time small flying insects become active. The diet of this species consists of insects and small fish. Bats of this species hunt about 1 meter above the water's surface. They roost in small groups mainly at caves and tree holes near water edges. In urban areas, they roost under bridges and covered drains.

Local Status and Range: Fairly common and widespread in Singapore.

(Image Source: Chan Kwok Wai**)**

Whiskered Myotis

Scientific Name: *Myotis muricola*
Other Names: Nepalese Whiskered Bat, Wall-Roosting mouse-eared Bat
Conservation Status: Least Concern

Size: Weight: Up to 5.5g, Head-Body Length: , Forearm Length: Up to 3.8g

Identification: Whiskered Myotis has dark brown to dark grey upperparts and pale grey underparts. This bat has a blunt snout, small eyes and pointy ears. The wing membrane of this bat almost completely encloses the tail.

Ecology and behavior: This insectivorous bat is known to roost in young, rolled up banana leaves.. These bats usually feed during the first two hours after sunset and the last two hours before the sun rises.

Local Status and Range: Whiskered Myotis are common and widespread in Singapore in all habitats except urban areas. This species is the most common species along the trails of various reserves.

(Image Source: Tan Kok Hui)

Javan Pipistrelle

Scientific Name: *Pipistrellus javanicus*
Other Names: None
Conservation Status: Least Concern

Size: Weight: 3-22g ,Head-Body Length: 4-5.5cm , Forearm Length: 3.1-3.2cm

Identification: This species of bat is a medium-sized Pipistrelle. It has a chestnut colored bat with dark brown wings and rounded ears which are furless. It has a short muzzle. The Javan Pipistrelle is significantly smaller than the other species of Pipistrelle found in Singapore (Narrow-winged Pipistrelle)

Ecology and behavior: The Javan Pipistrelle roosts in small groups.

Local Status and Range: This species is very rare in Singapore. It was thought to be extinct until one individual of this species was sighted on 25 June 2009 on the window of Ayer Rajah Crescent, in the Ayer Rajah Industrial Park. This species has been rediscovered in Singapore after 131 years.

(Image Source: Wildlife Singapore)

Narrow-winged Pipistrelle

Scientific Name: *Pipistrellus stenopterus*
Other Names: Malaysian Noctule,
Conservation Status: Least Concern

Size: Weight: 14-18g, Head-Body Length: 5.9-6.5cm , Forearm Length: 2.8-3.2cm

Identification: The Narrow-winged Pipistrelle has dark chocolate-brown upperparts and underparts with black-brown wings, face and ears. As its name suggests, this species of bat has narrow wings.

Ecology and behavior: This insectivorous bats roost in hollow trees, plantations and roofs of buildings in rural areas. Narrow-winged Pipistrelle is a gregarious species.

Local Status and Range: This species is rare in Singapore. BTNR is the best place to sight the Narrow-Winged Pipistrelle.

(Image Source: Archana Subramanian**)**

Asiatic Lesser Yellow House Bat

Scientific Name: *Scotophilus kuhlii*
Other Names: Yellow House Bats
Conservation Status: Least Concern

Size: Weight: 20-22g, Head-Body Length: 7cm, Forearm Length: 4.8-5.2cm
Identification: Asiatic Lesser Yellow House Bats have light brown to yellow fur on upperparts and underparts. It has a dog-like face with a blunt muzzle and large pointy ears. This bat's long tail is enclosed in a membrane between its hind legs.

Ecology and behavior: This species of bat roosts in fairly large colonies of several hundred induviduals in hollow trees and attics or abandoned buildings.

Local Status and Range: This species is very common in Singapore and is fairly widespread.

(Image Source: Atish Banerjee**)**

Lesser Bamboo Bat

Scientific Name: *Tylonycteris pachypus*
Other Names: Flat Headed Bat
Conservation Status: Least Concern

Size: Weight: 1.4-5.2g, Head-Body Length: 4cm, Forearm Length: 2.4-2.8cm

Identification: The Lesser Fruit Bat is one of the smallest mammals in the world. It has fur which varies in color from golden or cinnamon to dark brown. The under sides are paler. This bat has a flattened had with triangular ears and a short snout.

Ecology and behavior: Males mainly roost alone or in small groups of up to 6 induviduals. Females roost in groups of about 5 induviduals although larger groups of up to 38 induviduals have been recorded. Lesser Bamboo bats may frequently roost with Greater Bamboo Bats. These bats roost in slits in bamboo trees.

Local Status and Range: Quite rare. There was one confirmed individual in BTNR. However, due to the presence of Greater Bamboo Bats, it is complicated to identify this species of bat.

(Image Source: Udo Schroter)

Greater Bamboo Bat

Scientific Name: *Tylonycteris robustula*
Other Names: None
Conservation Status: Least Concern

Size: Weight: 4.6-5g, Forearm Length: 2.5-2.9cm

Identification: As its name suggests. the Greater Bamboo Bat is larger than the Lesser Bamboo Bat which is the main distinction between the two species. It has dark brown to greyish brown fur on upperparts. Wings are blackish.

Ecology and behavior: This species of bat feeds on insects. They roost in narrow slits in bamboo trees. The Greater Bamboo Bat normally emerges from its roost twice every night to hunt- once at dusk and once at dawn.

Local Status and Range: This species is fairly common and widespread in Singapore especially in the CCNR and BTNR.

(Image Source: Bat Consultancy)

Rodents

Rodents are the most common type of mammals in the world, accounting for about 40% of all mammal species. Squirrels, mice, rat, beaver and porcupine are some common examples of rodents. There are about 14 species of rodents in Singapore which largely consists of rats and squirrel.

Rodents are characterized by a pair of incisors on both upper and lower jaws. They are relatively small mammals with short limbs. The diet and social systems vary significantly. Some rodents, especially mice and rats are pests and are attracted by spoiled food which has not been disposed of properly.

Mice and Rat
Asian House Mouse
Scientific Name: *Mus castaneus*
Other Names: None
Conservation Status: Least Concern

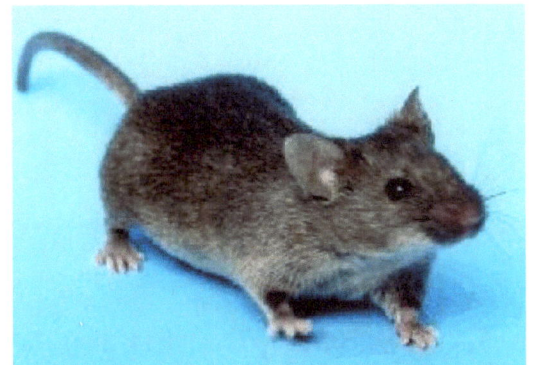

Size: Weight: 10-25g,   Head-Body Length: 7.5-10cm, Tail Length: 5-10cm

Identification: The Asian House Mouse is the only species of mice in Singapore. Wild house mice vary in color from light brown to dark brown. These mice have fairly less fur.

Ecology and behavior: House rats are mainly solitary but may live in small groups of 2-3 induviduals. These rats are nocturnal.

Local Status and Range: Very common especially in areas with lot of food scrapes especially in hawker centers and restaurants which do not dispose food scrapes properly. They can be seen sometimes in parks.

(Image Source: Wikipedia)

Asian House Rat
Scientific Name: *Rattus tanezumi*
Other Names: Tanezumi Rat
Conservation Status: Least Concern

Size: Weight: 200g , Head-Body Length: 22cm , Tail Length: 22cm

Identification: Upperparts are olive-grey while underparts are lighter. The dark tail is almost completely naked. The house mouse has black eyes and relatively large ears.

Ecology and behavior: The Asian House rat is very adaptable. These rats live in groups of 2-3 induviduals.

Local Status and Range: Very common in urban areas.

(Image Source: Melvin Yap**)**

Rajah Spiny Rat

Scientific Name: *Maxomys rajah*
Other Names: Brown Spiny Rat
Conservation Status: Vulnerable

(Image Source: Melvin Yap**)**

Size: Weight: 71-218g , Head-Body Length: 138.1-218cm Tail Length: 142-210cm

Identification: The Rajah Spiny Rat has brown upperparts and a white belly. In adult rats, there is a black midline across the belly. It has a pointed snout and short limbs. The top of the tail is dark while the bottom is pale. There are many spines throughout the body of this rat.

Ecology and behavior: The Brown Spiny Rat is nocturnal and solitary.

Local Status and Range: This rat is rare and is restricted to BTNR and CCNR.

Malaysian Wood Rat

Scientific Name: *Rattus tiomanicus*
Other Names: Malayan Field Rat
Conservation Status: Least Concern

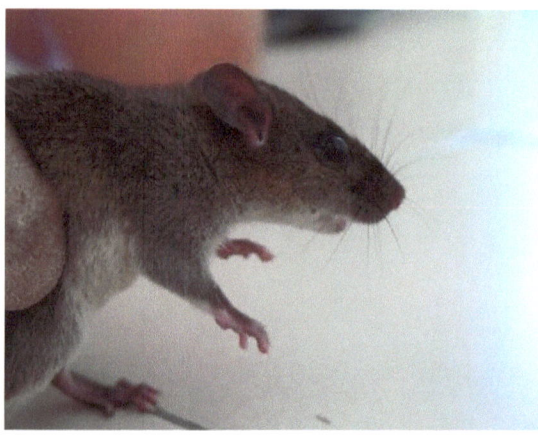

Size: Weight: 55-150g , Head-Body Length: 14-19cm, Tail Length: 15-20cm

Identification: Easily identifiable by white underparts and olive-brown upperparts. There are black guard hairs scattered on the upperparts. This rat differs from the Annandale's Rat by having sleek fur. Also the Malayan Wood Rat has smooth fur with occasional spines unlike the Annandale's Rat.

Ecology and behavior: This species of rat is nocturnal. These rats are good climbers but also spend quite some time foraging on the ground.

Local Status and Range: This species is rare in Singapore.

(Image Source: Jon Hall)

Polyhesian Rat

Scientific Name: *Rattus exulans*
Other Names: Pacific Rat
Conservation Status: Least Concern

Size: Weight: Up to 65g, Head-Body Length: Up to 14cm, Tail Length: Up to 16cm

Identification: Upperparts of this rat varies from greyish-brown to reddish brown. The fur on the upperparts is very spiny. The underparts are light grey. This rat has a dark, long tail.

Ecology and behavior: Polyhesian rats are nocturnal Males are solitary while females live in small groups.

Local Status and Range: This species of rat is the third most common rat species in Singapore and is fairly widespread. Urbanization is leading to an increase in the population of Polyhesian Rats

(Image Source: John Cassin**)**

Annandale's Rat

Scientific Name: *Rattus annandalei*
Other Names: Annandale's Sundaic Rat, Singapore Rat
Conservation Status: Least Concern

Size: Head-Body Length: Up to 22cm, Tail Length: Up to 27cm

Identification: Annandale's rat has pale yellow underparts and greyish brown fur on its upperparts. The tail of this rat is quite long and almost furless. This rat has medium sized eyes and a pointed snout.

Ecology and behavior: Annandale's rat is nocturnal and solitary. This rat is terrestrial.

Local Status and Range: Not very common in Singapore. Its range is restricted to BTNR and the CCNR.

(Image Source: Jon Hall**)**

Brown Rat

Scientific Name: *Rattus norvegicus*
Other Names: Common Rat, Street Rat, Wharf Rat and Norway Rat
Conservation Status: Least Concern

Size: Weight: 250g (F), 350G (M), Head-Body Length: 25cm, Tail Length: <25cm

Identification: The Brown Rat is a fairly large rat which is dark brown in color. Compared to the house rat, the black rat has a blunter muzzle.

Ecology and behavior:. Brown Rat lives in small groups of 2-3 induviduals. The Brown rat is more terrestrial than most other species of rats.

Local Status and Range: Quite common in urban areas of Singapore.

(Image Source: Christine Lee**)**

Squirrels

Variable Squirrel

Scientific Name: *Callosciurus finlaysonii*
Other Names: Finlayson's Squirrel
Conservation Status: Least Concerned

Size: Weight: 250g, Head-Body Length: 21cm, Tail Length: 22-24cm,

Identification: The variable squirrel has a distinct red-brown coat on the upperparts with white/cream colored underparts, face and sides. The upperparts can vary from light red to dark brown, hence its name.

Ecology and behavior: This diurnal mammal live either solitarily or in pairs.

Local Status and Range: This is an introduced species. There is a small population in Bidadari. Unlikely to be seen anywhere else.

(Image Source: Rushen**)**

Slender Sunda Squirrel

Scientific Name: *Sundasciurus tenuis*
Other Names: None
Conservation Status: Least Concerned

Size: Weight: 120-140g, Head-Body Length: 13-16cm, Tail Length: 12-13cm

Identification: The Slender Sunda Squirrel is Singapore's smallest squirrel. It has brown upperparts with greyish or brownish underparts. It has a long but slender tail and orange patch around its eyes and ears. These squirrels are significantly smaller and slender than the plantain squirrel.

Ecology and behavior: This nocturnal squirrel is fairly social, living in groups of 10 induviduals. These squirrels are arboreal.

Local Status and Range: Not very common in Singapore. They are mostly found in the CCNR and BTNR. There is a separate population found in Botanical Gardens.

(Image Source: Benjamin**)**

Horsfield's Flying Squirrel

Scientific Name: *Iomys horsfieldii*
Other Names: Javanense Flying Squirrel
Conservation Status: Least Concern

Size: Weight: Up to 165g, Head-Body Length: Up to 19cm, Tail Length: Up to 18cm

Identification: The upperparts of this squirrel are brown. Under the patagium is orange of whitish. The tail is orange to reddish.

Ecology and behavior: Flying squirrels do not 'fly" but rather glide through the air using their gliding membrane. These nocturnal squirrels normally live in pairs.

Local Status and Range: Quite rare in Singapore. It is fairly widespread in the CCNR and can be found in BTNR as well.

(Image Source: John Gerrard Keulemans**)**

Red-Cheeked Flying Squirrel

Scientific Name: *Hylopetes spadiceus*
Other Names: None
Conservation Status: Least Concerned

Size: Weight: Up to 157g , Head-Body Length: 19cm, Tail Length: 15 cm

Identification: This squirrel has rust colored markings on a dark-grey upperparts and white underparts with orange tinges. Cheeks are orange-brown. It has an orange tail and a white margin on its gliding membrane.

Ecology and behavior: The Red-Cheeked Flying Squirrel is both arboreal and terrestrial. This squirrel is nocturnal.

Local Status and Range: This species is very rare in Singapore and is restricted only to BTNR.

(Image Source: Wildlife Singapore**)**

Shrew-faced Ground Squirrel

Scientific Name: *Rhinosciurus laticaudatus*
Other Names: Long-Nosed Squirrel
Conservation Status: Near Threatened

Size: Weight:11.5-16g , Head-Body Length: 19-23cm, Tail Length: 11-17cm

Identification: As its name suggests, the Shrew-faced Ground Squirrel has a shrew like face with a pointed muzzle. It has a short and bushy tail. This squirrel has dark brown upperparts and whitish underparts.

Ecology and behavior: This squirrel is solitary and spends most its time on the ground. The Shrew-faced Ground Squirrel is very secretive and nests in log hollows.

Local Status and Range: This species was once very common in Singapore but is now very rare. It can be seen only in BTNR.

(Image Source: Amit Dutta**)**

Plantain Squirrel

Scientific Name: *Callosciurus notatus*
Other Names: Oriental Squirrel, Tricolored Squirrel
Conservative Status: Least Concerned

Size: Weight: 150-280 grams, Head Body Length: 17-22cm, Tail Length : 16-21 cm

Identification: Easily identifiable by brown coat. It has two white stripes along the side and an orange belly. It has a rather fluffy tail.

Ecology and behavior:. It generally lives in pairs. This is a diurnal mammal.

Local Status and Range: This is Singapore's most common squirrel. It can be found in most forested areas around Singapore and sometimes in parks with lot of tree cover.

(Image Source: Atish Banerjee)

Porcupine
Malaysian Porcupine

Scientific Name: *Hystrix brachyura*
Other Names: Himalayan Porcupine
Conservation Status: Least Concern

Size: Weight: 0.7kg-2.4kg , Head-Body Length: 63-72cm , Tail Length: 6-11cm

Identification: The Malayan Porcupine is a fairly large rodent with sharp quills. Quills are black and white or yellow in color. The quills are organized in a rigid structure. It has large, stocky brown legs.

Ecology and behavior: Like most porcupine species, Malaysian Porcupines are nocturnal and live either solitary or in pairs.

Local Status and Range: The Malayan Porcupine is not very common. Like many other mammal species in Singapore, it was thought to be extinct before being rediscovered again. There have been few records of these porcupines in PT and PU.

(Image Source: Rushenb)

Shrews

Shrews are small mammals which are quite similar to moles. Although shrews look like mice with a long nose, they are not rodents and are an entirely different order. The teeth of shrews wear down over time whereas for rodents have a two pairs of growing Shrews are very small mammals. These terrestrial mammals are omnivorous.

There are about 385 species of shrew worldwide out of which 2 are found in Singapore, including the largest shrew in the world- the Asian House Shrew

Asian House Shrew
Scientific Name: *Suncus murinus*
Other Names: Monkey Shrew, Asian musk shrew, Grey Musk Shrew
Conservation Status: Least Concern

Size: Weight: 50-60g ,Head-Body Length: 10-16cm, Tail Length: 4.5-10cm

Identification: Easily identifiable by its short and thick tail and large pink ears. It has a pointy snout. The color of the fur varies from grey to reddish grey.

Ecology and behavior: The house shrew is nocturnal, mainly active at dusk.

Local Status and Range: Very common in urban areas but rarely seen due to its nocturnal behavior.

(Image Source: L Shyamal**)**

Southeast Asian White-toothed Shrew
Scientific Name: *Crocidura fuliginous*
Other Names: Coal Shrew, Southeast Asian Shrew
Conservation Status: Least Concern

(Image Source: J.B. Blosson)

Size: Weight: 11.5-16g ,Head-Body Length: 7-10cm , Tail Length: 6-9cm

Identification: The Southeast Asian White-Toothed Shrew is the smallest shrew in Singapore. It has dark grey to blackish fur with sliver gloss. It has a thin tail.

Ecology and behavior: This shrew mainly feeds on insects and is mostly terrestrial. This nocturnal shrew is very secretive

Local Status and Range: Very rare. This shrew is restricted to the CCNR.

Tree-Shrews

Tree-shrews are small mammals native to Southeast Asia. Despite its name, tree-shrews are not related to shrews. In fact, they are more closely related to primates. Furthermore, many species are not completely arboreal. Terrestrial species tend to be larger than the arboreal shrews.

There are 20 species of tree-shrews worldwide but in Singapore there is only one- the Common Malayan Tree-Shrew

<u>Common Malayan Tree-Shrew</u>

Scientific Name: *Tupaia glis*
Other Names: None
Conservation Status: Least Concern

Size: Weight: 190g, Head-Body Length: 13-21cm, Tail Length: 12-20cm

Identification: This is one of the largest tree -shrew in the world. It has a dark-greyish bushy tail and white underparts. Upperparts can vary from reddish-brown to grey or black. The common tree-shrew has a white stripe on each shoulder.

Ecology and behavior: The Common Tree-Shrew is a diurnal mammal. They are mainly solitary and induviduals of the same gender are very territorial and are often involved in aggressive fights. Although these tree-shrews are adept climbers, they prefer to foliage on the ground.

Local Status and Range: Quite common especially in the CCNR and BTNR

(Image Source: Stavven Tupia**)**

Marine mammals

Marine mammals are aquatic mammals (mammals which partially or entirely live in water) such as whales, sea otters, and dolphin manatees etc. which require a marine ecosystem to survive in. These mammals may partially or entirely depend on a marine ecosystem for survival. There are approximately 115 species of marine mammals globally out of which. Although Singapore is surrounded by the Indian Ocean which is rich in marine life, it has only 6 confirmed species of marine mammals. This is mainly due to the large amounts of ship activity along the coast of Singapore.

Indo-Pacific Finless Porpoise
Scientific Name: *Neophocaena phocaenoides*
Other Names:
Conservation Status: Vulnerable

Size: Weight: 45kgs-72kg, Head-Body Length: 1.6m-2.2m

Identification: The Indo-Pacific Porpoise is the only porpoise species in the world which does not have a dorsal fin. Full grown adults are mostly dark-grey in color. Juveniles are almost completely black. Porpoise are smaller than dolphin. They differentiate from dolphins by their spade shaped teeth.

Ecology and behavior: The Indo-Pacific Finless Porpoise generally solitary or live in small groups. However large groups of about 100 induviduals have been recorded . These porpoise are active swimmers.
Local Status and Range: This species is a rare mammal which has been spotted a few times east of the coast of Changi.

(Image Source: remmikkiのブログ)

Indo-Pacific Humpback Dolphin (Chinese)

Scientific Name: *Sousa chinensis*
Other Names: None
Conservation Status: Near Threatened

Size: Weight: 250-283kg, Head-Body Length: 1.8-3m

Identification: The Indo-Pacific dolphin is a medium sized dolphin which can vary in appearance depending on where it's from. The ones found in Singapore are white with dark spots. These dolphins may appear pink due to blood circulation under the skin. This dolphin is identifiable by the hump on its back. Juveniles are black.

Ecology and behavior: Like most dolphins, the humpback dolphins are fairly social and live in small pods of 3-7 induviduals. There have been records of pods of up to 25 induviduals.

Local Status and Range: This is the most common species of dolphin in Singapore. It has been spotted regularly in SS.

(Image Source: Takor Adee)

Indo-Pacific Bottlenose Dolphin

Scientific Name: *Tursiops aduncus*
Other Names: None
Conservation Status: Data deficient

Size: Weight: Up to 230kg, Head-Body Length: Up to 2.6m

Identification: The Bottlenose Dolphin is greyish in color and has a large, stocky body. The long dorsal fin of this dolphin is quite dark grey in color. A sharp crease separates the dolphin's short beak from the forehead. The underside of this dolphin is very pale and for some induviduals, spotted.

Ecology and behavior: This dolphin is one of the friendliest dolphin species in the world. Bottlenose Dolphins are very active mammals.. Pods generally have about 5-15 induviduals but sometimes can be significantly larger

Local Status and Range: This is the second most common aquatic mammal in Singapore. This species has been frequently in the SS and near PU and PT.

(Image Source: Aude Steiner)

Irrawaddy Dolphin

Scientific Name: *Neophocaena phocaenoides*
Other Names: None
Conservation Status: Vulnerable

(**Image Source:** C. Berjeau)

Size: Weight: 90-130kg , Head-Body Length: 1.7-2.75m

Identification: The Irrawaddy Dolphin varies In color from dark blue-grey to pale blue. Its underside is significantly lighters. his dolphin is blunt-headed and beakless. It is similar to the Finless Porpoise except much larger and having a small dorsal fin.

Ecology and behavior: The Irrawaddy Dolphin very rarely comes out of water, although it does spit out water quite regularly and noisily. They generally live in small families of 2-3 with the pod occasionally having up to 15 induviduals.

Local Status and Range: This species is not very common. It has been sighted a few times in the SS

False Killer Whale

Scientific Name: *Pseudorca crassidens*
Other Names: None
Conservation Status: Data Deficient
Size: Weight: 1,200kg (F), 2,200kg (M) , Head-Body Length: 5.1m (F), 6.2m (M)

Identification: The False Killer Whale is the largest aquatic mammal in Singapore. This whale is uniformly dark grey with a white colored 'W' on its chest. It has a very large dorsal fin. This whale has a long slender head.

Ecology and behavior: The False Killer whale is very social mammal living in pods of 10-50 (sometimes 100) induviduals. They are active swimmers which feed on smaller cetaceans.

Habitat: Deep, warm offshore waters.

Local Status and Range: Very rare in Singapore. The carcass of a dead False Killer Whale has been found a couple of times in 1994 and 2015.

(**Image Source:** Luis Dias)

Dugong

Scientific Name: *Dugong dugon*
Other Names: Sea Cow
Conservation Status: Vulnerable

Size: Weight: 250-420kg , Head-Body Length: 2.5-4m

Identification: The dugong is a fairly large marine mammal. The upper body of a dugong is brownish grey while the underparts are whitish. The dugong's body has a similar shape to a dolphin but its head is similar to that of a seal or a walrus. Males have tusk-like incisors and heavy scarring on its body.

Ecology and behavior: Dugongs are very secretive mammals. Dugongs live in small pods with 2-6 induviduals.

Local Status and Range: Not very rare in Singapore. It has been spotted on numerous occasions in Check Jawa on PU

(Image Source: Julien Willem**)**

Even-toed Ungulates

Even-toed Ungulates are hoofed mammals which have two weight-bearing toes on each foot. They either have no other toes or significantly smaller toes on their feet. Generally, even-toed ungulates are herbivorous barring a few species. They are gregarious with varying social structures. Males of numerous species are solitary.

There are approximately 220 species of even-toed ungulates worldwide out of which 5 are found in Singapore.

Sambar Deer

Scientific Name: *Rusa unicolor*
Other Names: None
Conservation Status: Vulnerable

Size: Weight: 130-230kg (F), 180-270 (M,) Head-Body Length: 160-210cm , Tail Length: 22-35cm

Identification: Sambar deer is one of the largest deer in Asia. They have a shaggy-brown coat. The ears and tail of Sambar are relatively large. Only males have antlers which are three-tined. Males are much larger than females.

Ecology and behavior: Sambar deer are nocturnal mammals which are mostly active from dusk to dawn. Sambars are non-gregarious mammals. Full grown adult males are solitary. Sub adult males from bachelor herds. Females live in small herds with their offspring.

Local Status and Range: Sambar Deer are rare in Singapore with an estimated population of less than 20 induviduals in the CCNR. Sambar Deer became extinct in Singapore. They were reintroduced into Singapore in 1990

(Image Source: N. A. Naseer)

Lesser Mouse-Deer

Scientific Name: *Tragulus kanchil*
Other Names: Lesser Malay Chevrotain or Kanchil
Conservation Status: Least Concerned

(Image Source: Chan Kwok Wai**)**

Size: Weight: 2-2.5kg , Head-Body Length: 42-49cm, Tail Length: 6-9cm

Identification: The Lesser Mousedeer is significantly smaller than the Greater Mousedeer. It is identifiable by its reddish brown coat, pale underparts and three white stripes on its neck. Males have tiny canines. The tail of mouse deer is generally tucked inside the deer.

Ecology and behavior: The Lesser Mouse-Deer is mainly diurnal. This solitary mammal is very shy.

Local Status and Range: This species is rare in Singapore and their range is restricted to the CCNR and BTNR.

Greater Mouse-deer

Scientific Name: *Tragulus napu*
Other Names: Greater Malayan Chevrotain or Napu
Conservation Status: Least Concerned

Size: Weight: 5-8kgs, Head-Body Length: 70-75cm , Tail Length: 8-10cm

Identification: This is an extremely small mammal with a rounded body. Rear legs are longer than front legs. On the upperparts, the coat is orange and the sides are fairly pale. It is larger than the Lesser Mouse-Deer. Furthermore, the Greater Mouse-Deer has five throat stripes compared to three on the Lesser Mouse-Deer

Ecology and behavior: The Greater Mouse-Deer is a nocturnal mammal. Otherwise, its behavior is similar to its more common cousins

Local Status and Range: Greater Mouse deer are very rare and are only found in PU. The Greater Mouse-Deer was thought to be extinct but was rediscovered in 2009 in PU

(Image Source: Chan Kwok Wai**)**

Wild Boar

Scientific Name: *Sus Scrofa*
Other Names: None
Conservation Status: Least Concern

Size: Weight:200kg , Head-body Length: 150cm-200cm, Tail Length: 20cm-30cm

Identification: Wild Boars are large and hairy forest pigs. Males have small tusks and are dark-grey/brown. Females are lighter brown. Until the age of six months, piglets have longitudinal stripes and have a very light brown coat.

Ecology and behavior: Wild Boars live in sounders (families) of 6-20 induviduals made of females and their young. Males are generally solitary. Wild Boars are very shy but can be aggressive when provoked. They are active at dawn and dusk.

Local Status and Range: Wild Boards are common in Singapore and can be found in the WC, CCNR, Changi, PT and PU.

(Image Source: Jerzy Strzelecki**)**

Colugo

Colugos are a group of gliding mammals. Despite being commonly known as a "flying lemur," colugos are in fact not lemurs and do not fly. They are the most capable gliding mammals. Colugos are arboreal and nocturnal. There are only two separate species of colugos in Singapore- the Philippines Colugo and the Sunda Colugo. The latter is fairly common in Singapore's rainforests.

Malaysian/Sunda Colugo

Scientific Name: *Galeopterus variegatus*
Other Names: Malaysian/Sunda Flying Lemur
Conservation Status: Least Concern

Size: Weight: 1-2kgs, Head-Body Length: 32cm-45cm, Tail Length: 17-27cm

Identification: The Sunda Colugo is one of the two species of Colugo found in the world. It has red-brown to a greyish fur. Undersides are pale colored. The most distinct feature of these mammals is its kite-shaped membrane which surrounds its entire body and is visible during flight.

Ecology and behavior: The Malaysian Colugo is mostly nocturnal and arboreal. When it senses danger, it generally freezes on the same spot or crawls to safer areas while the threat exists.

Local Status and Range: Colugos are common in Singapore and can only be found in the CCNR and BTNR.

(Image Source: Lip Kee Yap**)**

Pangolins

Pangolins are rare scaly anteaters. They have thick scales which they use to protect themselves against predators by curling up in balls, hiding the softer parts of the body.. These shy creatures are nocturnal.

There are 8 species of pangolin, 4 in Asia and 4 in Africa. There is 1 species of pangolin in Singapore.

Sunda Pangolin

Scientific Name: *Manis javanica*
Other Names: Javan Pangolin, Malaysian Pangolin
Conservation Status: Critically Endangered

Size: Weight: 8-10kg , Head-Body Length: 40-65cm,   Tail Length: 35-62cm

Identification: The pangolin has an elongated and streamlined body which is covered in thick scales. These scales vary in color from light yellow-brown to dark brown. Head and neck are not covered in scales.

Ecology and behavior: The pangolin is a shy nocturnal mammal which is generally solitary. The Sunda Pangolin is one of the most arboreal species of pangolin in the world. When threatened, pangolins will roll into a ball.

Local Status and Range: Very rare. It prefers dense primary and secondary forests such as CCNR and PU. Their range also extends to Bukit Batok, the WC Area and PT.

(Image Source: Wildlife Singapore**)**

Checklist of Mammals

	English Name	Scientific Name	Checklist	Additional Notes
1.	Banded Leaf Monkey	*Presbytis femoralis*		
2.	Crab-Eating Macaque	*Macaca fascicularis*		
3.	Sunda Slow Loris	*Nycticebus coucang*		
4.	Asian-Small Clawed Otters	*Aonyx cinerea*		
5.	Smooth Coated Otters	*Lutrogale perspicillata*		
6.	Leopard Cat	*Prionailurus bengalensis*		
7.	Large Indian Civet	*Viverra zibetha*		
8.	Malaysian Civet	*Viverra tangalunga*		
9.	Three-Striped Palm Civet	*Arctogalidia trivirgata*		
10.	Common Palm Civet	*Paradoxurus hermaphroditus*		
11.	Common Fruit Bat	*Cynopterus brachyotis*		
12.	Cave Nectar Bat	*Eonycteris spelaea*		
13.	Dangger-toothed Long-Nosed Bats	*Macroglossus minimus*		
14.	Dusky Fruit Bat	*Penthetor lucasi*		
15.	Malayan Flying Fox	*Pteropus vampyrus*		
16.	Glossy Horseshoe Bat	*Rhinolophus lepidus*		
17.	Greater Woolly Horseshoe Bat	*Rhinolophus luctus*		
18.	Trefoil Horseshoe Bat	*Rhinolophus trifoliatus*		
19.	Bicolored-Leaf Nosed Bat	*Hipposideros bicolor*		
20.	Malayan False Vampire	*Megaderma spasma*		
21.	Lesser Sheath-Tailed Bat	*Emballonura monticola*		
22.	Black-Bearded Tomb Bat	*Taphozous melanopogon*		
23.	Naked-Rumped Pouch Bat	*Saccolaimus saccolaimus*		
24.	Malaysian Slit-faced Bat	*Nycteris tragata*		
25.	Greater Naked Bat	*Cheiromeles torquatus*		
26.	Hardwicke's Woolly Bat	*Kerivoula hardwickii*		
27.	Brown Tube-nosed Bat	*Murina suilla*		
28.	Horsfield's Large Footed Myotis	*Myotis horsfieldii.*		
29.	Grey Large Footed Myotis	*Myotis 'adversus'*		
30.	Whiskered Myotis	*Myotis muricola*		
31.	Javan Pipistrelle	*Pipistrellus javanicus*		
32.	Narrow Winged Pipistrelle	*Pipistrellus stenopterus*		
33.	Asiatic Lesser Yellow House Bat	*Scotophilus kuhlii*		
34.	Lesser Bamboo Bat	*Tylonycteris pachypus*		
35.	Greater Bamboo Bat	*Tylonycteris robustula*		
36.	Asian House Mouse	*Mus castaneus*		
37.	Asian House Rat	*Rattus tanezumi*		
38.	Rajah Spiny Rat	*Maxomys rajah*		
39.	Annandale's Rat	*Rattus annandalei*		

40.	Polynesian Rat	*Rattus exulans*		
41.	Brown Rat	*Rattus norvegicus*		
42.	Malaysian Wood Rat	*Rattus tiomanicus*		
43.	Asian House Shrew	*Suncus murinus*		
44.	Southeast Asian White-Toothed Shrew	*Crocidura malayana*		
45.	Common Tree Shrew	*Tupaia glis*		
46.	Variable Squirrel	*Callosciurus finlaysonii*		
47.	Plantain Squirrel	*Callosciurus notatus*		
48.	Shrew-faced Ground Squirrel	*Rhinosciurus laticaudatus*		
49.	Slender Sunda Squirrel	*Sundasciurus tenuis*		
50.	Red-Cheeked Flying Squirrel	*Hylopetes spadiceus*		
51.	Horsfield's Flying Squirrel	*Iomys horsfieldii*		
52.	Malayan Porcupine	*Hystrix brachyura*		
53.	Indo-Pacific Finless Porpoise	*Neophocaena phocaenoides*		
54.	Indo-Pacific Humpback Dolphin	*Sousa chinensis*		
55.	Indo-Pacific Bottlenose Dolphin	*Tursiops aduncus*		
56.	Irrawaddy Dolphin	*Orcaella brevirostris*		
57.	Dugong	*Dugong dugon*		
58.	False Killer Whale	*Pseudorca crassidens*		
59.	Sambar	*Rasa unicolor*		
60.	Greater Mousedeer	*Tragulus napu*		
61.	Lesser Mousedeer	*Tragulus kanchil*		
62.	Wild Boar	*Sus scrofa*		
63.	Sunda Colugo	*Galeopterus variegatus*		
64.	Sunda Pangolin	*Manis javanica*		
65.				
66.				
67.				

Bibliography

Adee, Takor. *Indo-Pacific Humpbacked Dolphin*. Digital image. *Wikipedia*. Wikimedia Foundation, 4 Apr. 2016. Web. 19 July 2016. <https://en.wikipedia.org/wiki/Indo-Pacific_humpbacked_dolphin>.

Asian Palm Civet. Digital image. *Animals Adda*. N.p., 11 July 2013. Web. 16 July 2016. <http://animalsadda.com/asian-palm-civet/>.

Baker, Nick. "Small Mammals of Southeast Asia." *Ecology Asia*. N.p., n.d. Web. 19 July 2016.
Website

Banerjee, Atish. *Plantain Squirrel*. Digital image. *Facebook*. Facebook, 4 July 2016. Web. 16 July 2016. <https://www.facebook.com/profile.php?id=100009185391944&sk=photos&collection_token=100009185391944:2305272732:5>.

Banerjee, Atish. *Small-Clawed Otter*. Digital image. *Wildlife of Singapore*. Blogger, 23 Feb. 2016. Web. 16 July 2016. <http://wildofsg.blogspot.sg/search?updated-min=2015-01-01T00:00:00-08:00&updated-max=2016-01-01T00:00:00-08:00&max-results=4>.

Banerjee, Atish. *Yellow House Bat*. Digital image. *Photoblog*. Blogger, 4 June 2016. Web. 16 July 2016. <http://anophotoblog.blogspot.sg/2015/07/pula-ubin-live-update.html>.
Digital Image

Bat Consultancy. *Greater Bamboo Bat*. Digital image. *New Page 0*. N.p., n.d. Web. 18 July 2016. <http://www.batconsultancy.co.uk/Greater bamboo bat.htm>.

"Bat Fact." *Reddit*. Reddit, 18 Aug. 2015. Web. 18 July 2016. <https://www.reddit.com/r/BatFacts/comments/3eg4zz/this_pitcher_plant_nepenthes_hemsleyana_has>.

"Bat." *Wikipedia*. Wikimedia Foundation, n.d. Web. 19 July 2016. <https://en.wikipedia.org/wiki/Bat>.

Benjamin. *Slender Squirrel*. Digital image. *Wikipedia*. Wikimedia Foundation, Dec. 2009. Web. 16 July 2016. <https://en.wikipedia.org/wiki/Slender_squirrel>.

Berjeau, C. *Irrawaddy Dolphin*. Digital image. *Wikipedia*. Wikimedia Foundation, 31 Jan. 2012. Web. 18 July 2016. <https://en.wikipedia.org/wiki/Irrawaddy_dolphin>.

Bicolored Leaf-nosed Bat. Digital image. *Mammals' Planet*. Sheet Zoom Image, n.d. Web. 18 July 2016. <http://www.planet-mammiferes.org/drupal/en/node/40?indice2=Photos%2FVolants%2FRhinolo%2FHippBic6.jpg>.

Blossom, J.B. *White Toothed Shrew*. Digital image. *Archive BVI*. BVI, 2010. Web. 18 July 2016. <http://bvi.rusf.ru/taksa/s0000/s0000364.htm>.

"Blyth's Horseshoe Bat." *New Page 0*. N.p., n.d. Web. 20 July 2016. <http://www.batconsultancy.co.uk/Blyths%20horseshoe%20bat.htm>.
Website

"Carnivore." *Wikipedia*. Wikimedia Foundation, n.d. Web. 19 July 2016. <https://en.wikipedia.org/wiki/Carnivore>.

Cassin, John. *Pacific Rat*. Digital image. *Mammal's Planet*. Sheet Zoom Image, n.d. Web. 19 July 2016. <http://www.planet-mammiferes.org/drupal/en/node/40?indice2=Photos%2FRongeur%2FMyomo%2FMurine%2FRattExu5.jpg>.

"Cave Nectar Bat." *Wikipedia*. Wikimedia Foundation, n.d. Web. 20 July 2016. <https://en.wikipedia.org/wiki/Cave_nectar_bat>.

Chua, Jareas. *Slow Loris*. Digital image. *Vertebrates of Asia, Facebook Group*. Facebook, 30 Dec. 2014. Web. 15 July 2016. <https://www.facebook.com/groups/782082785163572/>.

"Common Palm Civet - Paradoxurus Hermaphroditus." *Common Palm Civet - Paradoxurus Hermaphroditus*. N.p., n.d. Web. 20 July 2016. <http://www.blueplanetbiomes.org/common_palm_civet.htm>.

Dusky Fruit Bat. Digital image. *Mammal's Planet*. Sheet Zoom Image, n.d. Web. 19 July 2016. <http://www.planet-mammiferes.org/drupal/en/node/40?indice2=Photos%2FVolants%2FPterop%2FPentLuc6.jpg>.

Dutta, Amit. *Shrew-faced Ground Squirrel*. Digital image. *Pintrest*. Pintrest, 2009. Web. 20 July 2016. <https://www.pinterest.com/pin/570831321489654798/>.

"EDGE of Existence." *EDGE of Existence*. Royal Chater, n.d. Web. 19 July 2016. <http://www.edgeofexistence.org/mammals/species_info.php?id=1410>.

Ellis, Susan. *Nycteridae*. Digital image. *Wikipedia*. Wikimedia Foundation, 4 Feb. 2011. Web. 19 July 2016. <https://en.wikipedia.org/wiki/Nycteridae>.

"Greater Bamboo Bat." *Tylonycteris Robustula*. N.p., n.d. Web. 20 July 2016. <http://www.bio.bris.ac.uk/research/bats/China%20bats/tylonycterisrobustula.htm>.

"Greater Mousedeer." *Wikipedia*. Wikimedia Foundation, n.d. Web. 20 July 2016. <https://en.wikipedia.org/wiki/Greater_mouse-deer>.

Hall, Jon. *Mammal Watching Around the World*. Digital image. *Mammal Watching around the World*. N.p., n.d. Web. 20 July 2016. <http://www.mammalwatching.com/index.html>.

Horsfield's Myotis. Digital image. マレーシア. N.p., n.d. Web. 20 July 2016. <http://fruitbat.jp/otherbats/teminnkuhoohigekoumori/content/15k_8160916_large.html>. Digital Image

Hui, Tan Kok, and Eddy Lee. *Whiskered Myotis*. Digital image. *Singapore Wild Animals*. Blogger, 31 Dec. 2012. Web. 17 July 2016. <http://sgwildanimals.blogspot.sg/2012/12/bats.html>.

Joshi, Aditiya. *Black-bearded Tomb Bat*. Digital image. *Wikipedia*. Wikimedia Foundation, 1 June 2012. Web. 19 July 2016. <https://en.wikipedia.org/wiki/Black-bearded_tomb_bat>.

Keulemans, John Gerrad. *Javanese Flying Squirrel*. Digital image. *Wikipedia*. Wikimedia Foundation, n.d. Web. 16 July 2016. <https://en.wikipedia.org/wiki/Javanese_flying_squirrel>.

Kingston, Tigga. *Murina Suilla*. Digital image. *Vimeo*. N.p., 2 Feb. 2009. Web. 20 July 2016. <http://www.vimeoinfo.com/video/3046413/murina-suilla>.

Kinsey, Beth. "Polyenesian Rat." N.p., n.d. Web. 20 July 2016. <https://aardwolfpestkare.com/archives/Polynesian_Rat.pdf>. Kvartalynov, Paul. *Rhinolophus Luctus*. Digital image. *: Cettia*. N.p., 15 Dec. 2012. Web. 20 July 2016. <http://cettia.livejournal.com/52117.html>.

"Large Flying Fox." *Wikipedia*. Wikimedia Foundation, n.d. Web. 19 July 2016. <https://en.wikipedia.org/wiki/Large_flying_fox>.

"Large Indian Civet." *Wikipedia*. Wikimedia Foundation, n.d. Web. 20 July 2016. <https://en.wikipedia.org/wiki/Large_Indian_civet>.

Lee, Christine. "Pest Control in Buildings and Offices in Singapore." *Pest Control Singapore*. Pest Control Singapore, n.d. Web. 18 July 2016. <http://www.pestcontrolsg.com/articles/rats-and-pest-control-in-buildings-and-office.html>.

Lee, Eddy. *Banded Leaf Monkey*. Digital image. *Singapore Wild Animal*. N.p., 13 Apr. 2011. Web. 14 July 2016. <http://sgwildanimals.blogspot.sg/2012/12/primates.html>.

Leong, Tzi Ming, and Kelvin Lim. "NOTEWORTHY MICROCHIROPTERAN RECORDS FROM BTNR AND CCNR." *Nature in Singapore* (2009): 83-90. 25 Feb. 2009. Web. 20 July 2016. <http://lkcnhm.nus.edu.sg/nis/bulletin2009/2009nis83-90.pdf>.

Leong, Tzi Ming, Mishak Surani, and Kelvin Lim. "THE NARROW-WINGED PIPISTRELLE." (2010): 159-65. National University of Singapore, 26 Aug. 2010. Web. 20 July 2016. <http://lkcnhm.nus.edu.sg/nis/bulletin2010/2010nis159-165.pdf>.

"Leopard Cat." *Wikipedia*. Wikimedia Foundation, n.d. Web. 20 July 2016. <https://en.wikipedia.org/wiki/Leopard_cat>.

"Lesser Long-Tongued Fruit Bat." *Encyclopedia of Life*. Encyclopedia of Life, n.d. Web. 20 July 2016.

Lim, Kelvin, and Leong Tzi Ming. "New Record of the Horsfield's Large-footed Myotis in Singapore." *Singapore Biodiversity Records* (2014): 106-07. 25 Apr. 2014. Web. 20 July 2016. <http://lkcnhm.nus.edu.sg/nis/sbr2014/sbr2014-106-107.pdf>.

Long-tongued Nectar Bat. Digital image. *Wikipedia*. Wikimedia Foundation, 1 Jan. 2015. Web. 19 July 2016. <https://en.wikipedia.org/wiki/Long-tongued_nectar_bat>.

Lundrigan, Barbara, and Juile Harris. "Viverra Tangalunga (Malayan Civet)." *Animal Diversity Web*. University of Michigan, 200. Web. 20 July 2016. <http://animaldiversity.org/site/accounts/information/Viverra_tangalunga.html>.

"Malayan Field Rat." *Wikipedia*. Wikimedia Foundation, n.d. Web. 20 July 2016. <https://en.wikipedia.org/wiki/Malayan_field_rat>.

"Malayan Flying Lemur." *The Animal Files*. N.p., n.d. Web. 19 July 2016.

"Malayan Porcupine." *Wikipedia*. Wikimedia Foundation, n.d. Web. 20 July 2016. <https://en.wikipedia.org/wiki/Malayan_porcupine>.

"Mammals- Species List- Wildlife in Singapore." *National Parks*. NParks, n.d. Web. 20 July 2016. <https://www.nparks.gov.sg/biodiversity/wildlife-in-singapore/species-list/mammal>.

"Marine Mammal Research Lab." *Marine Mammal Research Lab*. National University Singapore, n.d. Web. 20 July 2016. <https://www.tmsi.nus.edu.sg/mmrl/>.

Mariomassone. *Oriental Civet*. Digital image. *Wikipedia*. Wikipedia, 30 Dec. 2011. Web. 15 July 2016. <https://en.wikipedia.org/wiki/File:Oriental_civet.jpg>.

Menon, Vivek. *Indian Mammals: A Field Guide*. 1st ed. Vol. 1. Gurgaon: Hachette Bok India Pvt., 2014. 110+. Print.

Midori, Sakurai. "File:Ngarai Sianok Sumatran Monkey.jpg." - *Wikimedia Commons*. Wikipedia, 23 Nov. 2005. Web. 15 July 2016. <https://commons.wikimedia.org/w/index.php?curid=1368270>.

Murinae. Digital image. *Wikipedia*. Wikimedia Foundation, n.d. Web. 17 July 2016. <https://en.wikipedia.org/wiki/Murinae>.

Naseer, N. A. *Sambar Deer*. Digital image. *Wikipedia*. Wikimedia Foundation, 27 Nov. 2007. Web. 17 July 2016. <https://en.wikipedia.org/wiki/Sambar_deer>.

"NParks' Flora and Fauna Web." *NParks' Flora and Fauna Web*. NParks, n.d. Web. 20 July 2016. <https://florafaunaweb.nparks.gov.sg/>.

"Oriental Small-clawed Otter." *Wikipedia*. Wikimedia Foundation, n.d. Web. 20 July 2016. <https://en.wikipedia.org/wiki/Oriental_small-clawed_otter>.

Patil, Sunny. *Leopard Cat*. Digital image. *Facebook*. Facebook, 6 Jan. 2016. Web. 15 July 2016.
<https://www.facebook.com/photo.php?fbid=10153413344062582&set=pb.702802581.-
2207520000.1468585587.&type=3&theater>.

Phil, M. *Asian Small-Clawed Otter*. Digital image. *Otter Joy*. N.p., 2005. Web. 16 July 2016.
<http://www.otterjoy.com/otterinfo/aonyx/cinereus/cinereus_habitat.html>.

Photographs from Fraser's Hill. Digital image. *Cicada Tree Eco-Place*. Cicada Tree Eco-Place, 23 Jan. 2011. Web. 15 July 2016.
<http://cicadatree.blogspot.sg/2011_01_01_archive.html>.

"Primate." *Wikipedia*. Wikimedia Foundation, n.d. Web. 19 July 2016. <https://en.wikipedia.org/wiki/Primate>.

Rajah Spiny Rat. Digital image. *Sheet Zoom Image*. Mammal's Planet, 1 Nov. 2010. Web. 17 July 2016. <http://www.planet-mammiferes.org/drupal/en/node/40?indice2=Photos%2FRongeur%2FMyomo%2FMurine%2FMaxoRaj2.jpg>.

"Remmikkiのブログ." *Remmikkiのブログ*. N.p., 6 June 2015. Web. 19 July 2016.
<http://blog.livedoor.jp/remmikki/archives/2015-06-19.html>.

Rusheb. *Finlayson's Squirrel*. Digital image. *Wikipedia*. Wikimedia Foundation, 25 Nov. 2012. Web. 16 July 2016.
<https://en.wikipedia.org/wiki/Finlayson's_squirrel>.

Rushenb. *Malayan Porcupine*. Digital image. *Wikipedia*. Wikimedia Foundation, 6 Nov. 2013. Web. 18 July 2016.
<https://en.wikipedia.org/wiki/Malayan_porcupine>.

Schroter, Udo. *Lesser Bamboo Bat*. Digital image. *Wikipedia*. Wikimedia Foundation, 28 Apr. 2013. Web. 17 July 2016.
<https://en.wikipedia.org/wiki/Lesser_bamboo_bat#/media/File:Lesser_Bamboo_Bat.JPG>.
Digital Image

Shyamal, L. *Asian House Shrew*. Digital image. *Wikipedia*. Wikimedia Foundation, 27 Nov. 2015. Web. 16 July 2016.
<https://en.wikipedia.org/wiki/Asian_house_shrew>.

"Smooth-coated Otter." *Wikipedia*. Wikimedia Foundation, n.d. Web. 20 July 2016. <https://en.wikipedia.org/wiki/Smooth-coated_otter>.

Steiner, Aude. *Indo-Pacific Bottlenose Dolphin*. Digital image. *Wikipedia*. Wikimedia Foundation, 2003. Web. 18 July 2016.
<https://commons.wikimedia.org/wiki/File:Tursiops_aduncus,_Port_River,_Adelaide,_Australia_-_2003.jpg>.

Strzelecki, Jerzy. *Eurasian Wild Boar*. Digital image. *Wikipedia*. Wikimedia Foundation, 10 May 2010. Web. 18 July 2016.
<https://en.wikipedia.org/wiki/Wild_boar#/media/File:Locha(js).jpg>.

Subramanian, Archana. *Batting for the Bat*. Digital image. *The Hindu*. The Hindu, 10 Oct. 2011. Web. 20 July 2016.
<http://www.thehindu.com/features/kids/batting-for-the-bat/article2520564.ece>.

Theo, Robert, and Subaraj Rajahurai. *Mammals, Reptiles and Amphibians in the Nature Reserves of Singapore- Diversity, Abundance and Disturbution* (1997): 361-68. Vertebrate Study Group, Nature Society (Singapore). Web.
<https://www.sbg.org.sg/images/4_4_Research_Gardens_Bulletin/4_4_49_2_pdf_Vol_49_Part_2_1997/4.4.49.2.11_y1997_V49P2_GBS_pg.353.pdf>.

TonTan Travel. *Large Indian Civet*. Digital image. *Wikipedia*. Wikimedia Foundation, 14 Nov. 2014. Web. 15 July 2016.
<https://commons.wikimedia.org/wiki/File:Large_Indian_Civet,_Viverra_zibetha_in_Kaeng_Krachan_national_park.jpg>.

Tupaia, Stavven. *Common Treeshrew*. Digital image. *Wikipedia*. Wikimedia Foundation, 18 Feb. 2007. Web. 16 July 2016.
<https://en.wikipedia.org/wiki/Common_treeshrew>.

Wai, Chan Kwok. *Large-footed Myotis - Myotis Spp*. Digital image. *Large-footed Myotis - Myotis Spp*. N.p., n.d. Web. 19 July 2016. <http://www.ecologyasia.com/verts/bats/large-footed-myotis.htm>.

Wai, Chan Kwok, Leong Tzi Ming, and K. Lim. "THE JAVAN PIPISTRELLE." *NATURE IN SINGAPORE* (2009): 323-27. National University of Singapore, 6 Aug. 2009. Web. 20 July 2016. <http://lkcnhm.nus.edu.sg/nis/bulletin2009/2009nis323-327.pdf>.

Wai, Chan Kwok. *Lesser Mousedeer*. Digital image. *Wildlife Singapore*. N.p., 19 Mar. 2015. Web. 18 July 2016. <http://www.wildsingapore.per.sg/fauna/facts/mousedeer_lesser.htm>.

Wai, Chan Kwok. *Uninvited Guest on Vesak Day*. Digital image. *The Lazy Lizard's Tales*. N.p., n.d. Web. 18 July 2016. <http://lazy-lizard-tales.blogspot.sg/2009/05/uninvited-guest-on-vesak-day.html>.

Wai, Chan Kwok. *Wildlife Singapore - Greater Mousedeer*. Digital image. *Wildlife Singapore*. N.p., 21 Feb. 2009. Web. 18 July 2016. <http://www.wildsingapore.per.sg/fauna/facts/mousedeer_greater.htm>.

Wai, Chan Kwok. *Wildlife Singapore-Mammals*. Digital image. *Wildlife Singapore-Mammals*. Wildlife Singapore, n.d. Web. 18 July 2016. <http://www.wildsingapore.per.sg/fauna/pages/mammals2.htm>.
Digital Image

"Wild Singapore." *Wild Singapore*. N.p., 1 July 2015. Web. 20 July 2016. <http://www.wildsingapore.com/>.

Willem, Julien. *Dugong*. Digital image. *Wikipedia*. Wikimedia Foundation, 1 July 2008. Web. 18 July 2016. <https://en.wikipedia.org/wiki/Dugong>.

"Woolly Horseshoe Bat (Rhinolophus Luctus)." *INaturalist.org*. INaturalist, n.d. Web. 20 July 2016. <http://www.inaturalist.org/taxa/40686-Rhinolophus-luctus>.

Yap, Francis. *Malaysian Flying Fox*. Digital image. *Facebook*. Facebook, 27 May 2016. Web. 16 July 2016. <https://www.facebook.com/photo.php?fbid=10209395405866721&set=a.1923486331475.111920.1371625899&type=3&theater>.

Yap, Lip Kee. *Sunda Flying Lemur*. Digital image. *Wikipedia*. Wikimedia Foundation, 18 June 2006. Web. 17 July 2016. <https://en.wikipedia.org/wiki/Colugo>.

Yap, Melvin. *Oriental House Rat*. Digital image. *Zipcode Zoo*. Zipcode Zoo, 20 July 2015. Web. 16 July 2016. <http://zipcodezoo.com/index.php/File:Rattus_tanezumi_1.jpg#filelinks>.

www.ingramcontent.com/pod-product-compliance
Lightning Source LLC
Chambersburg PA
CBHW041518280526
45792CB00004B/1292